PREDATOR

Written by Susan Mayes

Illustrated by Gary Boller

Phidal

Published in Canada by Editions Phidal
Henderson - An imprint of DK Publishing, Inc.
Copyright © 1997 Dorling Kindersley Ltd.

MEET THE PREDATORS

Predators hunt, kill, and EAT other animals. Think of sharp teeth, needlelike claws, and powerful jaws and you've got your average predator. Yikes!

T. re

There are really obvious examples like the long-dead dinosaur, *Tyrannosaurus rex*, or a lion. But what about that sweet, cuddly little creature at home that you call kitty? Yes...your beloved cat is a predator, too! (Sorry to break it to you like that!)

Predators come in all shapes and sizes, and with slight variations. Swimmers such as sharks and leopard seals use their lethal teeth to do away with their victims.

Fliers such as owls and bats come out at night to track down their evening meal.

Barn owl

Snakes slither in search of prey and kill using their poisonous bite, or by giving a suffocating hug (depending on the type of snake). You should see the size of some of the things they gulp down...ENORMOUS!

Boa constrictor

Then there are plants...yes, plants! Have you ever thought that they kill for food? Well...not all of them, but certain types live on a tasty diet of flies and other unsuspecting creatures that come their way.

Don't forget the mini-killers either. Ants and spiders are among the small predators you'll come across. Maybe not that frightening if you're an average human, but pretty scary if you're their next snack!

Venus flytrap

Tarantula

Now don't let any of this put you off. The sight of a mouse's tail hanging out of Kitty's mouth may not be all that appealing, but that's life ...that's nature! Prepare to be fascinated, gripped, and maybe even slightly appalled...but be warned...you may have trouble tearing yourself away!

PREHISTORIC KILLERS

Many millions of years ago, before your granny was born, dinosaurs roamed the Earth. Some were peaceful planteaters called *herbivores*, and others were hunting meateaters called *carnivores*. These meat-eating beasties chased and ate other dinosaurs, or fed on dead bodies that they found. Mmm-mmmm!

How thecodontians changed

BEFORE THE DINOSAURS

Before dinosaurs came on the scene, their crocodilelike ancestors, the thecodontians (pronounced theck-oh-don-tee-ons) were the VIPs. Over millions of years, these cumbersome creatures changed the way they moved their legs and became smaller and faster moving.

STAURIKOSAURUS

Staurikosaurus (store-rick-oh-saw-rus) was one of the first meat-eating dinosaurs. It sped along nimbly on its long back legs, in an upright position. It snapped up prey with its tooth-lined jaws.

Staurikosaurus *was about 6 ft 6 in (2 m) long.*

COMPSOGNATHUS

Compsognathus (comp-so-nay-thus) was one of the smallest
known meat-eating dinosaurs. Although the little fella
was 3 ft (1 m) long, a lot of this was tail.
Its body was about the size
of a chicken's.

*Compsognathus probably
ate little creatures such
as lizards or dragonflies.*

DEINONYCHUS

Deinonychus *(die-non-i-kus)*
was a gruesome beast!
It was 8-11 ft (2.4-3.4 m) long (not huge by dinosaur
standards) but boy, was it FIERCE! These dinosaurs
hunted in packs, leaping on an unsuspecting
plant-eater and slashing at it with their claws.

*Long arms
with three-
fingered
claws*

*Sicklelike claw on
second toe of foot*

TERRIBLE CLAW

The name *Deinonychus* means "terrible claw." The claw
behind the name is on
each back foot. These
vicious weapons were
held up out of the way
when the dinosaur ran.
They flicked forward
for slashing and
attacking. Ouch!

*Position when
not in use*

Position for attack

Introducing T. rex

Tyrannosaurus rex (or *T. rex* for short) was mighty big, mighty strong, mighty heavy, and mighty FEROCIOUS! It was the largest land-living meateater that we know about. Here are some fearsome facts about this big brute.

Last One Standing

T. rex lived a mere 65 million years ago. In fact, it was one of the last dinosaurs to become extinct (to die out). Scientists know when this happened, but they are not sure why. Something violent probably happened to change the world's climate.

The Biggest Beast

T. rex was the largest of the meat-eating dinosaurs. It was about 46 ft (14 m) long and 18 ft (6 m) tall. Imagine meeting THAT on your way home from school! Aaaagh!

What Legs!

T. rex's leg bones were thick to support its incredible weight. Powerful, rippling muscles helped this giant thunder along in pursuit of a meal.

Weedy Arms

For a muscly monster, *T. rex* had really scrawny arms. They were short, with two claws on each one. It probably used them to push itself up after taking a well-earned break from hunting and killing.

Gruesome Gnashers

The gaping mouth of *T. rex* was full of serrated teeth for tearing its victims apart. These knifelike weapons were as long as 7 in (18 cm), which is a little bigger than the height of this book. Ooh!

Eating Out

Most dinosaurs would have looked like a tasty snack to *T. rex*. However, some dinosaurs were harder to attack than others. *T. rex* would have had a tricky time fighting the armored planteater shown here.

Edmontonia
(Ed-mon-tone-ee-ah)

LIONS AND TIGERS

Lions and tigers are probably the best-known of the big cat family. These magnificent, powerful beasts are fantastic hunting machines.

Lion

DESIGNED FOR HUNTING

Big cats are perfectly (or should that be *purrfectly?*) designed for hunting, and the lion is no exception. It is intelligent, strong, and fast.

GROUP HUNTING

Lions live in Africa and in a small forest in India. They are the only cats that hunt in groups. Most of the hunting is done by the females. They have massive paws for swiping prey, and sharp teeth for snapping bones.

TIGER TERRITORY

Tigers live in lots of different parts of the world including the rain forests of Southeast Asia, and in freezing cold Siberia. The tiger is the biggest and most powerful of all the big cats.

NOT SO FAST!

Tigers cannot run fast for very long, but they make up for this with their great strength, attacking large prey without much problem. They are also good swimmers...handy for relaxing and keeping cool!

Tiger

Massive paws for swiping prey

HIDE AND SNEAK

A tiger's black and orange stripes match the patches of sun on the grass and trees, so the beast doesn't stand out. This helps it hide and sneak up on its prey without being seen. Surprise, surprise!

BELIEVE IT OR NOT...

Siberian tigers are the biggest tigers, weighing up to 845 lb (384 kg). They can jump 40 ft (12 m) – more than four times their body length!

MORE WILD CATS

Small wild cats are different from big ones because of their size...obviously! But another main difference is that they cannot roar. (Grrr-aah!) For more fascinating feline facts, read on...

EARLY CATS

The earliest fossil ancestors of the cat family come from about 50 million years ago. Another type of early cat was the saber-toothed cat. It had dagger-like teeth in its upper jaw.

Smilodon (smil-oh-don) – a saber-toothed cat that became extinct about 11,000 years ago

CHEETAHS

The cheetah is different from all other cats because it is better at running than leaping. When it is running at full speed, it can reach 60 mph (96 kph).

LEOPARDS

Leopards are secretive creatures, living alone and hunting mostly at night. They are agile climbers and can easily scale a vertical tree. Carrying dead prey up into the branches is no problem.

Lazing around is just the thing after a big meal.

JAGUARS

Jaguars hunt alone, killing creatures such as sloths, tapirs, and turtles. Although they can climb, they are much happier hunting at ground level and in water. River turtles and even crocodiles make particularly tasty snacks!

BELIEVE IT OR NOT...

A black panther is just a leopard with different coloring. It has spots, but you have to look really closely to see them among all the dark fur. (Careful though!)

PUMAS

Pumas (also known as cougars) search huge distances for their next meal. Once they have caught it, they may drag it 1,300 ft (400 m) to hide it from scavengers. Good idea!

THE GREAT WHITE SHARK

The mere mention of a great white shark can transform even the "bravest swimmer into a quivering wreck." But does this awesome, swimming predator deserve its reputation as a bloodthirsty killer? Read on and make up your own mind.

VITAL STATISTICS

At their largest, great white sharks can grow to over 20 ft (6 m) long. They can weigh more than 2 tons.

BELIEVE IT OR NOT....

One of the largest sets of great white shark jaws in the world is 22.5 in (57.5 cm) wide. You would have no trouble slipping in there quite comfortably!

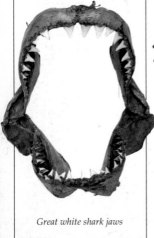

Great white shark jaws

MOVIE STAR STATUS

A great white shark was the star of a scary 1970s movie called *Jaws*. In the movie, it was responsible for killing unsuspecting swimmers, but in reality attacks on people are rare. Phew!

CRAFTY COLORING

This lethal creature's pale coloring helps it blend into the watery scenery and sneak up on its prey. From underneath, its white belly looks like a bright patch of sunlight on the water.

On the Menu

A great white shark's diet changes as it grows up. Young, small sharks like a tasty piece of fish. The older ones prefer a more varied menu, which includes seals, porpoises, sea lions, some sea birds, and even other sharks. Yikes!

Eye Eye

When a great white shark goes in for the kill, its eyes roll back in their sockets, so that the whites of the eyes show. This helps protect the vital eye parts from being scratched by the flailing victim.

Sharp, serrated tooth of a great white shark (actual size)

Model of a male great white shark

There are up to 400 species of shark lurking in the oceans of the world. Here are just a few fishy snippets to whet your appetite, with a killer whale thrown in for good measure.

Sixth Sense
Sharks have the same five senses as us humans – they can hear, see, taste, smell, and touch. But they also have special pores on their heads, which can sense electrical signals generated by swimming supper. Smart, huh?

Bendy Body
The leopard shark spends a lot of time lurking near the seabed. Its flexible body gives it a handy advantage when hunting, since it can turn around easily in small spaces. Nifty, huh?

Leopard shark

Hammerhead
The hammerhead shark got its name because it looks like it has swallowed a hammer! Its eyes are on the end of the protruding parts, and its nostrils are widely spaced at the front. This wide head is good at sensing nearby snacks.

Open mouth of a basking shark

BIG BASKER

The basking shark doesn't go in for big meals; it prefers snacking. It swims along with its big mouth wide open and filters all the tiny creatures out of the water. Every minute or so, it swallows its catch.

COOKIECUTTERS

The cookiecutter shark is a small creature with a nasty eating habit. It uses its lips to suck onto its chosen victim

(whales, seals, and dolphins are popular). Then it bites and swivels around, tearing off the flesh. Ouch!

KILLER WHALE

An adult male killer whale (or orca) can grow to 30 ft (9 m) long. It's a fearsome hunter and consumes anything from little fish to whales ten times its size. Gutsy or what?

There's nothing quite like a swim in the ocean...bobbing around on the crest of a wave. Next time you go for a dip, give a moment's thought to some of the hunters that roam the oceans of the world.

UGLY MUG

The deep-sea angler fish is no beauty, so it's just as well that it lurks in the dark depths of the ocean. Some species of angler fish lure their prey with a luminous spine. Then they clamp their victim in sharp-toothed jaws and swallow them whole! Greedy!

Big, stretchy belly has space for huge prey

EIGHT-ARMED HUNTER

At night, the common octopus sneaks up on its victim and pounces. It wraps its supper in its eight arms, injects its stomach juices into the creature, then sucks out the squishy flesh. Slurp!

Arms hold prey

Suckers grip rocks

FEELING BLUE

The blue-ringed octopus (shown here) could fit in a person's hand, but DON'T try it, as this little monster has a lethal bite. Look out for its warning system – blue-ringed spots appear on its skin if it is irritated, or when it is feeding. "Leave me ALONE!"

SQUID ATTACK!

Squid can grow big...1 ton big. That really is some GIANT! Sperm whales often have scars where squid suckers have zapped on to get a grip.

NEW GNASHERS

Wolffish

The wolffish crunches through the hard shells of sea urchins, mussels, and crabs with its fanglike teeth. When the front set of teeth are worn down, they are replaced by a new set of gnashers that grow in behind the first set.

ARCTIC ATTACKERS

In the freezing cold Arctic, a meal is not always easy to come by. Many animals that live there have to be ruthless killers to make sure that they get the food they need to survive.

POWERFUL HUNTER

The polar bear is the most powerful hunter in the Arctic. It lies patiently by a hole in the ice, waiting for a seal to come up for air. When the unsuspecting victim pops up, the bear swipes it with its huge paw and bites it at the back of the skull. End of story!

Hollow hairs trap warm air near body.

HUNTING PRACTICE

Polar bear cubs at play are a delightful sight. It's easy to forget that their games help them learn and practice the skills they need to become hunters, like their parents.

A MIXED MENU

A grizzly bear's diet changes at different times of the year, depending on what is available. Small mammals, fish, and insects are all popular, and plants are a healthy extra.

STEALTHY STOAT

The stoat (or ermine) looks sweet and furry, but it is really a merciless killer. It chases little rodents, called lemmings, through their underground tunnels. Vroom!

WICKED WOLVERINE

This fearsome creature is a relative of the stoat. It is heavily built and VERY strong. It has no problem killing its main prey – reindeer. Just look at those vicious teeth and claws!

Wolverine

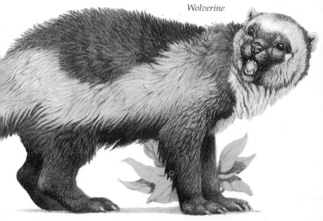

WOLVES

Wolves live in groups called packs, with up to 20 family members. They manage to survive in the freezing Arctic because of their thick fur and group-hunting habits.

CAMOUFLAGED COAT

Wolves living in the Arctic parts of North America and Eurasia often have a white coat. This cunning disguise lets them hunt against a snowy background without being seen by their prey. Boo!!

BELIEVE IT OR NOT...

A wolf can jump as far as 15 ft (4.5 m). It can also leap upward, sideways, and backward. What a nimble athlete!

HOWLING TOGETHER

Before a hunt, all the wolves in the pack have a good howling session, to show that they are ready for "the kill." One of them starts, then the others gradually join in. A-ooooh!

Canine Cuisine

Wolves mostly hunt large hoofed animals such as moose, caribou, and musk oxen. They run down their prey together in a team effort.

Special Features

A wolf is a superbly designed hunter. Here are a few features that make it so good at the job:

Ears hear sounds up to 2 miles (3 km) away. (Eyesight is poor!)

A keen nose smells when a live meal is in the area.

Powerful jaws are home to 42 teeth for gripping and tearing flesh.

A strong body and long legs are excellent for chasing prey.

DEADLY DOGS

There are about 37 species in the dog family. All members of the family are carnivores (meateaters), so bad luck for prey of all sizes! Here are a few morsels of information about wild dogs, for you to sink your teeth into.

AFRICAN HUNTING DOGS

These odd-looking creatures live on African grasslands, in big family packs. When they are hunting, their strong scent helps them keep in contact and their white-tipped tails make it easier to spot each other.

After a kill, the hunters regurgitate (vomit) bits of food for the puppies and the other dogs who stayed behind. Tasty!

LONE HUNTER

The red fox is one of the most common carnivores in the world. It has a taste for rodents and rabbits, so it helps keep down the numbers of these creatures in the wild.

Red fox

HOT FOX

The fennec fox lives in the Sahara desert and the Arabian desert. Keen eyes, a sensitive nose, and ENORMOUS ears help this little fox hunt on even the darkest desert night (it's too hot to hunt in the day). Phew!

COLD FOX

The Arctic fox's thick fur and furry feet help keep out the cold. It feeds on birds, which live on the ground, lemmings, and other small rodents. It can stand temperatures as cold as –58°F (–50°C). Brrrrrr!

Fennec fox

DINGOES

Dingoes are wild dogs that live in Australia. They gather into big packs to hunt large prey. Sheep and rabbits are popular supper specials.

Dingo

CUDDLY KILLERS

Now for the moment all you cat-lovers have been waiting for. It's time to feature that furry little bundle of fun...the domestic cat. A word of warning – don't be.TOO shocked by what follows!

WHY CATS HUNT

Domestic cats don't usually hunt because they are hungry. It's because chasing live food is a fun game that they enjoy playing. Well...it makes a change from hanging around on the windowsill.

WHAT'S ON THE MENU?

Basically, anything that moves is likely to be swiped by your darling pet. Creatures like birds and rodents are best for chasing though...so lock up your hamsters! If kitty proudly presents you with extra breakfast, try not to be angry. It's a prized gift showing that she thinks of you as an important part of her family. (Thanks, kitty!)

GETTING THE HANG OF IT

Cats learn how to hunt by watching what other cats do, and by trying it out for themselves. If a kitten has a nonhunting mother, then the chances are that it won't be destined for a life of mousing!

PLAY-FIGHTING This game helps them test their strength and learn new skills.

ESSENTIAL HUNTING SKILLS

Kitty approaches her victim by slinking stealthily along the ground.

She pauses to watch it, then slinks on again.

When she is close enough, Kitty prepares to jump. Her feet tread and her tail twitches.

She shoots forward and leaps on her prey, pinning it down.

PLAYING AROUND

Cats often play with their prey before killing it.

One bite with her sharp teeth and it's "good-bye Mr. Mouse!"

The game is much more fun (for the cat!) if the poor creature struggles between attacks. Sorry, but it's a fact of cat life!

Jungle Hunters

The jungles of the world are home to predators great and small. Tigers have already had their turn, and snakes and crocodiles are lurking a few pages on. It's time to feature a motley assortment of other jungle hunters who shouldn't be overlooked.

Water Dragons

Water dragons are lizards that live in the forests of Southeast Asia and Australia. They live mainly in trees growing near water, where they search for eggs and nestlings to eat. If they are disturbed, they drop into the water below. Wheeeeeee... splash!

Water dragon

The Giant Otter

A giant otter is happiest in the water. It makes its home in holes in the river bank or under tree roots. This big creature's favorite menu includes fish, eggs, water mammals, and birds.

THE MARBLED SCORPION

Although this fearsome little creature has a poisonous sting in its tail, this is mainly for defending itself. It overpowers the small creatures that it hunts using its jaws and front claws.

Marbled scorpion

GONE FISHING

The fishing bat (or bulldog bat) preys on fish. It skims low over the water and lifts them out with its sharp, hooked claws. It either eats its prey while flying (an impressive trick!) or carries it to its roost to dine in comfort.

SINISTER CENTIPEDE

The giant tiger centipede really ISN'T something you would like to meet on a ramble through the jungle. Its orange and black stripes warn that it is poisonous. It injects its victims with venom using the sharply tipped claws on its first pair of legs. Steer clear!

HUNGRY PLANTS

Insects make a tasty snack for many creatures, but they are also food for plants in some parts of the world. (Yes...plants!) If the soil is poor quality, the plants need the extra food to survive. They entice and trap creepy crawly victims for their next meal.

DEATH TRAPS
Pitcher plants have juglike traps at the ends of their leaves. Each one has a lid over the top to keep the rain out, and sweet nectar around the rim. Insects catching a whiff of the nectar land on the slippery rim, fall inside, and drown in the liquid at the bottom. Glug, glug...

Pitcher plant

Dead insects are slowly digested in liquid

A STICKY END
The leaves of sundew plants are covered in tiny hairs which make droplets of sticky, gluey stuff. An insect landing to investigate sticks to the hairs that fold over and trap it. Farewell little fly!

A WATERY GRAVE

Bladderworts are water plants that develop tiny bladders on their delicate leaves. If a little water creature passes by, a bladder snaps open and the creature gets sucked inside. Woosh!

SNAPPY KILLER

A Venus flytrap looks and smells attractive to an unwary insect. A safe landing place with a supply of nectar...what could be better? But within seconds of touchdown, the two halves of the leaf snap shut. If the plant senses that its victim contains protein, the trap closes fully and digestion starts. Yummy!

The damselfly lands on the trap.

The trap closes.

The Venus flytrap

Mini-Killers

There are many small-scale meateaters around the world that kill to survive, including one-third of insects. Take a look at these little beasties to see what they're up to.

Perilous Praying Mantis

The praying mantis is cunningly disguised in green, so it looks like a leaf. It grabs its prey with spiky front legs and slices through the doomed victim's body casing with its powerful, sharp jaws. Then it scoops out the innards. Mmm-mmm!

Praying mantis

Soup Again!

A diving beetle larva (that's the beetle in the early stages of its life) has a gruesome way of killing. It spears its prey with its pointed fangs and squirts juices into it, dissolving the victim's body into a soupy mush, which the larva then sucks up. Shloop, slurp!

Paralyzed Prey

Most hunting wasps are planteaters and only hunt prey to feed their young. The world's largest wasp, the tarantula hawk wasp, paralyzes a spider with her sting, then lays an egg on it. When it hatches, the grub feeds on the fresh, living meat. Yuck!

Adult hunting wasp

FEARSOME ANT

All ants have strong jaws, called mandibles, for chopping up food. The bulldog ant is a particularly fierce customer since it eats other insects. It has extra big mandibles which it uses for catching its victim and chopping it up into easy-to-eat pieces.

SPIDER SUPPERTIME

Who could forget spiders... those sinister scuttlers? Spiders the world over live on the creatures they catch. Many (but not all) of them trap their victims in a silky

Bulldog ant

web, inject them with paralyzing poison, then suck up the body juices. Easy when you know how!

BELIEVE IT OR NOT...

The pygmy shrew is no creepy crawlie, but it deserves a mention since it is one of the tiniest mammals. It dines on earthworms and other small creatures. It has to eat almost its own weight in food each day. Imagine that!

EAGLES

Eagles are the most powerful birds of prey. They have excellent eyesight, huge wings, and strong legs and feet. These special features help them hunt and capture their tasty victims.

Golden eagle

HOT AIR

Natural currents of hot air rise into the sky. They are called thermals. Eagles use these thermals to lift them higher into the air. Wheeee...

If you are a small, scurrying creature, it would be handy to know how to spot an eagle before it spots you! Keep an eye out for giveaway signs: wings with finger-like tips and a white tail.

MAGNIFICENT KILLERS

The golden eagle has huge talons (claws), a hooked beak, and really fantastic eyesight. When hunting, it soars high in the sky, searching for prey. Suddenly, it swoops and grabs a victim, killing it with its crushing claws.

Golden eagle

LAZY HUNTER

The bateleur eagle feeds mostly on carrion – that's dead and rotting flesh to you! It makes fierce attacks on other carrion-feeding birds and robs them of their "meal." However, it sometimes makes the effort and kills for itself.

Bateleur eagle

When angry or excited, it raises its crest.

HUGE HARPY

The harpy eagle lives in the rain forests of South Mexico to North Argentina. It is the largest eagle in the world and has feet the size of an adult's hand, so don't mess with this one! It uses its enormous talons to snatch prey, such as howler monkeys or sloths, from the branches.

Harpy eagle

MORE KILLER BIRDS

We all need to eat to survive, but look at the lengths that some birds go to, to catch their daily supply of food.

SICK SUPPER
The Andean condor is the world's heaviest bird of prey. It flies over the Andes looking for dead, sick, or wounded animals to eat. There is usually plenty of food around because living conditions there are difficult. That's handy!

DIVE, DIVE, DIVE!
The brown pelican is the only pelican that dives for food. When it spots its' fishy prey, it dives down into the water from as high as 50 ft (15 m). It scoops up food in the stretchy pouch under its beak, coming up to the surface to dine.

THE LANNER FALCON
The lanner falcon hunts and lives in the desert. It's partial to birds called sandgrouse and hovers in the sky, looking out for them. When it spots one, it swoops down, catching the creature in midair or on the ground.

Hooked beak rips flesh.

Lethal talons catch prey.

Leftovers

Predatory birds that feed
on other birds and small
mammals cannot chew their
food since they have no teeth.
To get rid of the undigested
bits of bone, fur, and feathers,
they vomit up pellets containing
the leftovers. Nice!

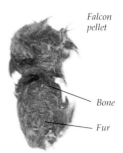

Falcon pellet

Bone

Fur

Believe It or Not...

The gannet is a sea bird that puts on an impressive
display when it goes fishing.
It folds its wings and plunges from as high as 100 ft
(30 m) to dive-bomb schools of fish in the water below.
That's some stunt!

Pirate Bird

The skua is a ruthless hunter with a reputation
as "pirate of the skies." It chases other birds
and forces them to vomit up their food
for it to eat. It also steals
the eggs
and young
of other birds,
as well as killing
ducks and gulls.
Boooo! Hiss!

Skua

NIGHT HUNTERS

Animals that come out at night are called *nocturnal* animals. Those which hunt live prey are specially developed for catching their evening snack in darkness...and that's without a flashlight!

OWLS

Most owls sleep in the day and hunt at night. Their brilliant eyesight and sharp hearing help them catch scurrying mice and small birds.

The barn owl has fringed feathers that muffle the sound of its moving wings, so small animals cannot hear it coming. Eeek!

Barn owl

ENORMOUS EYES

The bushbaby has huge eyes and ears to help it hunt at night. Its enormous eyes can see flying insects in the dark, and its sensitive ears can hear them. It clings to the branch with its back feet and stretches to snatch the flying midnight snack with its hands. Clever, huh?

Bushbaby

NIGHT MONKEY

The douroucouli, or night monkey, is the only monkey in the world to come out at night. It likes to eat fruit and leaves, but it also leaps from branch to branch, hunting for insects and other small animals.

HUNTING BY SOUND

Bats sleep during the day, hanging upside down by their feet. At night, they come out to hunt for insects. They make high-pitched sounds that bounce off flying insects, so they can home in on the echo and...crunch, slurp!

Bat

FURRY FIEND

The red-kneed tarantula lives in the rain forest. It stays in its silk-lined burrow in the day and comes out at night. It hunts insects and small creatures, which it paralyzes by injecting with venom. Lovely!

Sssssssnakes

Snakes are long, slithering, hissing, legless reptiles. They are ALL meat-eaters, but only about one-tenth of them are dangerous to people. Snakes live all over the world, except in very cold places, so if you're feeling weak in the knees...start packing those winter woollies!

Sensing Prey

Snakes have poor eyesight and hearing, but they make up for this in other ways. They have no external (outside) ears, but they can sense vibrations with an inner ear. Some snakes have little heat-sensitive holes in their lips for detecting warm-blooded prey. Uh-oh!

Believe It or Not...

Giant snakes can swallow REALLY big animals. If a constrictor eats something like a whole leopard (yes, a WHOLE leopard), it probably won't eat anything else for a year. Surprise, surprise!

BEASTLY BOA CONSTRICTOR

For those of you who like a gruesome tale, here are the details of how a boa constrictor consumes its prey.

The snake attacks its victim and clamps the wriggling creature in its jaws. Then it starts to coil around it, gripping tighter and tighter, suffocating it.

Once the victim's heart stops beating, the snake adjusts the animal's position so that it will slip down the throat easily.

The snake moves its flexible jaws from side to side, easing the animal down. Small creatures disappear quickly, but larger ones take an hour or more.

POISONOUS FANGS

Vipers, cobras, and sea snakes are among the most dangerous snakes of all. Their venomous fangs are at the front of their upper jaw and contain a poisonous cocktail that subdues victims, ready for killing.

Red spitting cobra ejects venom from tiny holes in fangs.

MAKE IT SNAPPY!

Crocodiles and their snappy relatives are an ancient group of animals related to the dinosaurs. They lurk around the tropical regions of the world.

SNAPPING SKULLS

Take a peek at the terrifying teeth in the skull of this snappy hunter... if you dare!

A crocodile's teeth are ideal for gripping and piercing, but pretty useless for slicing and chewing. It has to tear chunks of flesh off prey such as buffalo.

Nile crocodile

A QUICK BURST

Nile crocodiles can grow frighteningly big, but even the small ones can overpower and kill large animals, including people! They lurk in the watery depths for a lot of the time, but they put on a quick burst of speed to catch prey. They drag it underwater to drown it.

THE BIGGEST

The biggest crocodile in the world is the aggressive estuarine (or saltwater) crocodile. Some as long as 26 ft (8 m) have been recorded. If you want to avoid these beasties, steer clear of the area from southern India to northern Australia.

A NONCROCODILE SNAPPER

The alligator snapping turtle is a dangerous creature. It lies motionless on the riverbed with its mouth wide open. It is almost invisible to passing fish, except for a strange wormlike part on the end of its tongue. "Ah, food," the fish thinks as it gets up close, and...SNAP, gulp...gone!

Strong jaws slice fish in half.

LETHAL LIZARDS

There are over 3,000 species of lizard. Many of them are predators and feed on insects, mammals, birds, and other reptiles.

Basilisk lizards

RUNNING ON WATER

The basilisk (or Jesus Christ) lizard can run on water. Yes...run on water! It has large back feet with a flap of skin on its hind toes. This big surface area helps the lizard chase prey across water as well as across land. Wow!

EYED LIZARDS

The eyed lizard is a fast mover whose favorite foods are crickets and grasshoppers. It gives chase and grabs its victim in its jaws. A violent shake is all that it takes to stun the creature. Then the lizard passes the meal to the back of its throat with short, snapping movements.

FATTER WITH AGE

The tegu lizard starts life as a slim young thing, but it gets fatter as it gets older. This is because of all the birds, mammals, and other lizards that it eats. Burp!

Tegu lizard

THE BIGGEST LIZARD

The Komodo dragon is the largest living lizard in the world. It attacks animals such as wild boar, deer, and water buffalo, cutting off chunks of flesh with its serrated teeth. One captured giant was 10 ft 2 in (3.10 m) long and weighed 365 lb (165.6 kg). Yikes!

Chameleon

CAMOUFLAGE

Chameleons have another useful trick that helps them hunt successfully. They can change color to blend in with the background, so ambushing prey becomes much easier. This skill is also handy when avoiding being spotted by enemies. Pretty smart, huh?

FROGS AND TOADS

Frogs and toads belong to a group of animals called *amphibians* that typically live on land but breed in water. Their long back legs give them extra power to chase and catch the insects and other creatures that they feast upon.

WIDE-MOUTHED TOAD

The ornate horned toad has a huge mouth that is ideal for catching big insects, frogs, and mice. It sits and waits for "food" to come its way. Its camouflaged skin helps it blend into the background and surprise the next victim to pass by.

CREEPING TOADS

The common toad watches its prey closely. It even stalks it with movements like a cat's, when it hunts live food. Once it is close enough, it leans over, darts its tongue out, and snatches up the tasty morsel. It blinks as it swallows, since this helps push the food down. Gulp!

Common toad

HUNTER AND HUNTED

Poisondart frogs live in Central and South America and are very brightly colored. Although they are predators, they are also in danger of being hunted and eaten by other creatures. (Uh, oh!) The bright colors warn other predators that they are poisonous to eat, so "STAY AWAY!"

This spotted poison-dart frog comes from Costa Rica, Panama, and Columbia.

LOOK OUT!

White's tree frog has round, sticky toe-pads and feeds on anything that is small enough for it to swallow. It lives in forests, but it is also known to Australians because it lives in their water barrels and, believe it or not, in their bathrooms! So if you're down under, check down under before you get comfortable!

PREDATOR PUZZLE

Okay, smart alecs! So you've read all about those beastly predators. How many of the fascinating, fearsome facts have you managed to gobble up? Score two points for every correct answer, plus extra points where they are available.

1 A BLACK PANTHER IS REALLY A TYPE OF WHAT?

(a) Jaguar (b) Leopard (c) Puma

2 WHICH ARCTIC KILLER ENJOYS A MAIN DIET OF REINDEER?

(a) Wolverine
(b) Polar bear
(c) Grizzly bear

3 WHERE ARE A SHARK'S SENSORY PORES?

(a) Along its back
(b) On its head
(c) On its fins

4 WHICH SHARK GULPS DOWN SMALL CREATURES EVERY FEW MINUTES?

(a) Basking shark (b) Leopard shark (c) Cookiecutter shark

5 WHICH MEMBER OF THE DOG FAMILY IS THE ODD ONE OUT? (SCORE AN EXTRA POINT IF YOU CAN SAY WHY.)

(a) Wolf (b) African hunting dog (c) Red fox

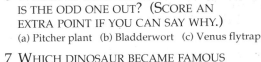

6 **WHICH OF THESE MEAT-EATING PLANTS IS THE ODD ONE OUT? (SCORE AN EXTRA POINT IF YOU CAN SAY WHY.)**
(a) Pitcher plant (b) Bladderwort (c) Venus flytrap

7 **WHICH DINOSAUR BECAME FAMOUS FOR ITS SLASHING CLAWS?**
- (a) Deinonychus
- (b) Staurikosaurus
- (c) Tyrannosaurus rex

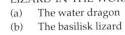

8 **WHICH IS THE LARGEST LIZARD IN THE WORLD?**
- (a) The water dragon
- (b) The basilisk lizard
- (c) The Komodo dragon

9 **WHICH BIRD HAS A REPUTATION AS "PIRATE OF THE SKIES"?**

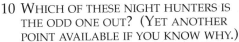

(a) Golden eagle   (b) Andean Condor   (c) Skua

10 **WHICH OF THESE NIGHT HUNTERS IS THE ODD ONE OUT? (YET ANOTHER POINT AVAILABLE IF YOU KNOW WHY.)**
- (a) Bat
- (b) Bushbaby
- (c) Owl

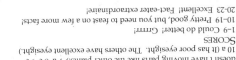

ANSWERS
1 b 2 a 3 b 4 a 5 c (It is a lone hunter. The others are pack hunters.) 6 a (It doesn't have moving parts like the other plants.) 7 a 8 c 9 c 10 a (It has poor eyesight. The others have excellent eyesight.)

SCORES
1-9 Could do better! Grrrr!
10-19 Pretty good, but you need to feast on a few more facts!
20-23 Excellent! Fact-eater extraordinaire!

INDEX

Picture credits:
Planet Earth Pictures/M&C Denis-Hout 10b; Wild Images Ltd./Dutcher Film Productions 20b; Bruce Colman Ltd./John Shaw 21; Oxford Scientific Film/Kathie Atkinson 31a.

Additional photography :
Jane Burton, Peter Chadwick, Andy Crawford, Geoff Dann, Colin Keaton, Frank Greenaway, Dave King, Karl Shone, Kim Taylor, Harry Taylor, Jerry Young.

Every effort has been made to trace the copyright holders. Henderson Publishing Ltd. apologizes for any unintentional omissions and would be pleased, in such cases, to add an acknowledgment in future editions.